History

It is extremely difficult to ascertain the precise date when Cockatiels were first brought to Great Britain and Europe. When some of the early books on birds are examined Cockatiels will be found mentioned briefly and

The bright yellow head and crest are exclusively masculine characteristics in the Normal Grey Cockatiel. Photo courtesy of Vogel park Walsrode.

often under names different from their present one. An excellent hand tinted color plate is to be found in Volume X of *The Naturalist Library* which was published about 1840. In this volume they are given the name of Red-cheeked Nymphious (*Nymphious Novae Hollandiae*) Wagler but the color plate establishes their identity beyond any doubt. A color plate of the Budgerigar under the name of *Undulated Nanodes* also appears although in this case it is quite unrecognizable as the bird we know so well today. This seems to indicate, strange though it may seem, that Cockatiels were better known to the ornithologist of that period than was the Budgerigar. The following extract from *Volume X* is rather interesting as it shows how limited was the knowledge of Australian birds '...It does not appear to be a numerous species, as few specimens have yet found their way into our museums, and no detailed accounts of its natural history have hitherto been recorded. It is a native of New Holland, of what particular district we are ignorant. It is likely that this bird and its congeners will constitute the rasorial type of this sub-family. In the lengthened tail feathers of this genus an analogy or distant affinity to the Ring Parrakeets, with which the illustrations are concerned, may be traced.'

Cassell's Book of Birds, Volume 1, which was translated from Dr. Brehm's original text and published in the latter part of the nineteenth century has an excellent print of a number of Cockatiels by a water hole in their native habitat. They are given a similar Latin name, *N. Hollandicae,* as in *The Naturalist Library* but their common name is given as the *Corella.*

After giving an accurate description of both cocks and hens, Dr. Brehm writes'...Gould, whom we have to thank for a full description of the Corella, found this beautiful bird in great numbers in the interior of Aus-

The author, Annmarie Barrie.

Front endpapers: *Photo by M. Gilroy.*
Back endpapers: *Photo by L. van der Meid.*

Title page: *A pair of Normal Grey Cockatiels enjoying their freedom outside the confines of a cage. Photo by N. Richmond.*

A Beginner's Guide To
Cockatiels

Written By
Anmarie Barrie

Contents

1. **History, 7**
2. **Housing, 15**
3. **Feeding, 23**
4. **Breeding, 27**
5. **Normal Colors, 35**
    Cock, 36; Hen, 36; Immature Birds, 36
6. **Albino Cockatiels, 39**
    Cock, 40; Hen, 40; Immature Birds, 40
7. **Pearled Cockatiels, 43**
    Cock, 44; Hen, 44; Immature Birds, 44
8. **Cinnamon Cockatiels, 45**
    Cock, 47; Hen, 47; Immature Birds, 47
9. **Pied Cockatiels, 49**
    Cock, 50; Hen, 50; Immature Birds, 50
10. **Dilute Cockatiels, 51**
    Cock, 52; Hen, 52; Immature Birds, 52
11. **Other Color Varieties, 53**
12. **The Pet Cockatiel, 57**

© 1986 by T.F.H. Publications, Inc. Distributed in the UNITED STATES by T.F.H. Publications, Inc., 211 West Sylvania Avenue, Neptune City, NJ 07753; in CANADA by H & L Pet Supplies Inc., 27 Kingston Crescent, Kitchener, Ontario N2B 2T6; Rolf C. Hagen Ltd., 3225 Sartelon Street, Montreal 382 Quebec; in ENGLAND by T.F.H. Publications Limited, 4 Kier Park, Ascot, Berkshire SL5 7DS; in AUSTRALIA AND THE SOUTH PACIFIC by T.F.H. (Australia) Pty. Ltd., Box 149, Brookvale 2100 N.S.W., Australia; in NEW ZEALAND by Ross Haines & Son, Ltd., 18 Monmouth Street, Grey Lynn, Auckland 2 New Zealand; in SINGAPORE AND MALAYSIA by MPH Distributors (S) Pte., Ltd., 601 Sims Drive, #03/07/21, Singapore 1438; in the PHILIPPINES by Bioi-Research, 5 Lippay Street, San Lorenzo Village, Makati Rizal; in SOUTH AFRICA by Multipet Pty. Ltd., 30 Turners Avenue, Durban 4001. Published by T.F.H. Publications, Inc. Manufactured in the United States of America by T.F.H. Publications, Inc.

The lacy pattern of the body and wing feathers are beautifully displayed in this photo of a Pearled Cockatiel. Photo courtesy of Vogel park Walsrode.

tralia. On the coast it is rare in comparison with the thousands seen on the plains of the interior, and in eastern Australia it seems to be more numerous than in the western parts of that Continent. In summer the Corellas make their nests near the Hunter and Peel rivers, and other streams running north, if they can find suitable trees. After the breeding season they assemble in innumerable flocks, which cover whole tracts of country, or alight in hundreds upon the overhanging branches of the gum trees....They devour grass seed, but cannot live without water, and, thereby, must remain in the neighbourhood of a stream...'

The first book in which Cockatiel keeping and breeding in captivity is described at length is *Budgerigars and*

Cockatiels by C.P. Arthur and published by *Cage Birds* in the early 1920's. It will be noted here that Cockatiel is spelt thus, "Cockateel" and that the Latin name given as *Calopsittacus novae-hollandioe*. Other common names mentioned in the book are Crested Ground Parrakeet and the Grey and Yellow Top-knotted Parrot. The natural history and color descriptions are based on that previously given by John Gould. Part of the opening paragraph contains further names by which these birds were known,"...With the exception of the north-east corner of Queensland, they range practically over the whole of Australia. Quarrion and Top-knot Parrakeet are their Australian names..."

A later book, *Foreign Birds for Beginners* by Westley T. Page, also published by *Cage Birds* uses the "double e" spelling and the same Latin name. However, Allen Silver's *The Parrot Book* published in the 1930's by Marshall Press Limited, which contains a brief description of many Parrot-like birds, uses the present name Cockatiel with the Latin name *Leptolophus hollandious*. In *Birds of Western Australia* by Serventy and Whittel, published in 1948, the same names are used as given by Allen Silver. Other names that have been used in Australia are Cockatoo Parrot and Weero.

Alec Brooksbank of Keston Foreign Bird Farm fame also quotes the same Latin name as Allen Silver in his *Foreign Birds for Garden Aviaries,* again published by *Cage Birds* in the 1950's. A little later in 1956 E. J. Boosey, a partner of Alec Brooksbank, used the present day spelling with the current Latin name of *Nymphicus hollandicus.*

In *"Australian Parrots in Captivity"* by Alan Lendon published in 1951 by the Avicultural Society there are

Facing page: Cockatiels love company.
Photo by L. van der Meid.

Correct way of holding your pet Cockatiel. A female, shown here, will require careful handling when she is bred and about to lay eggs. Photo by Dr. E. J. Mulawka.

some very interesting notes on the Cockatiel. I quote "...Distribution: Occurs over most of Australia, is commoner in the northern parts and is rarely seen near the coast in the south....Variations: Several subspecies have been described, but minor variations are common in a number of birds from any given locality, especially in the hens." The observations of Alan Lendon confirm those of older writers when they state that although there were slight color variations they were not enough to create definite sub species. "...It is well known that the cock Cockatiel shares the duties of incubation, sitting from early morning to late afternoon when the hen carries on for the remainder of the twenty-four hours.

Both sexes feed the young but I cannot recall ever having seen a cock feed his mate.

It has always been my opinion that the Cockatiel is more closely related to the Cockatoos than the true Parrots, partly on account of both sexes brooding and partly because the sexual differences in the plumage which are, to my mind, analogous to those which occur in the black Cockatoos, especially in the two Red-tailed species...

A cock Cockatiel when first introduced to a hen, especially if he has led a bachelor existence for some time, usually indulges in a rather comical display consisting of a series of rather absurd looking hops whilst following the hen along the ground, and accompanied by a low warbling variant of the usual shrill call note. Apart from this preliminary courtship, I have never seen a cock display to his mate, and although devoted to each other and indulging frequently in mutual preening, they are quite easily consoled after the loss of a mate and readily pair up when a newcomer is introduced."

It has not been possible to track down the date or place when the first breeding in captivity took place. When the writings of the early nineteenth century ornithologists and aviculturists are examined it would appear that Cockatiels must have been breeding in aviaries soon after their importation during the first half of that century. It was soon discovered that Cockatiels settled down to captive conditions very easily and were of a docile and friendly nature. A further point in their favor was they made agreeable companions for Budgerigars in colony aviaries. Not only were they good companions for Budgerigars but they also lived on most peaceful terms with small Waxbills and Finch-like species.

13

Cockatiels have been widely bred in small numbers for many years and it is only within the last few decades that their culture has become so much more widespread and specialized. As more birds become available for the general market and color mutations started to appear, their breeding has become much more widespread in many countries. They are now popular in their normal and mutant colors as aviary birds and have definitely established themselves as household pets, many of which have been taught to talk.

With patience, one can teach a Cockatiel to talk. No one can guarantee that a particular Cockatiel will learn to speak, but you can always try. Photo by E. Goldfinger.

2.

Housing

Being birds of some 33 cm (13 in) in overall length, Cockatiels will need to be housed in similar but larger structures than Budgerigars or Canaries. Single pet birds can be very well housed in wooden cages or all-

This type of cage is intended to house a single Cockatiel. Breeders are best kept in larger cages or, better yet, in an aviary. Photo by W. Wallace.

Caged Cockatiels should be released regularly to allow them to use and exercise the flight muscles. Photo by W. Wallace.

wire square or round Parrot cages. Breeding pairs can be housed in large cages, pens, indoor aviaries, and flighted or unflighted garden aviaries according to the space available to the breeder. Large stock cages will be required for giving the birds being raised for exhibition purposes their initial training. The vast majority of Cockatiels of all colors are extremely friendly to Budgerigars and Finch-like species which make them ideal inhabitants for mixed aviaries housing either large or small collections. Although Cockatiels are quite large birds they are not nearly so active in their flying habits as are some of the smaller Parrot-like species, but they must have a reasonable amount of flying space if they are to be maintained in a fit, healthy, vigorous condition.

The majority of breeders find that Cockatiels reproduce to their greatest capacity when housed in aviaries, and particularly so those birds having access to an outside flight. Although Cockatiels do not fly as much or as frequently as many other species of Parakeets, they must nevertheless have a reasonable amount of room for exercise. As a general rule the size of the flight should be about twice the length of the sleeping quarters, so if these were 2m (6 ft 6 in) long, the flight should be 4m (13 ft) in length. The actual size of an aviary will of course be controlled by the amount of space available and the number of birds kept by the breeder, and it can be adjusted to fit into any given area. Breeders realize that overcrowding of accommodation is undesirable, and particularly so in a breeding aviary if successful results are to be obtained. The density of the population of a colony breeding aviary of Cockatiels, however, can be greater than that of most other Parakeets because of their particularly amenable nature.

It is not practical to try to grow shrubs or bushes in a Cockatiel aviary because the birds will quickly kill the growing shoots by their habit of gnawing. Grasses of various kinds, however, can be successfully grown on the floor of a flight and they will provide green food and a playground for the birds. It is necessary that the birds have an opportunity to gnaw and the perches in the flight should, if possible, be made from branches of fruit, hazelnut, willow, alder, elm, hawthorn, sloe, or similar trees. Should any of these natural perches be unobtainable by the breeder then dowels can be used but small twigs from the above trees should be given to the birds from time to time. It is very important for the well being of the birds that they have an opportunity to consume a certain amount of green wood to give them the cellulose they need especially during breeding periods.

The supply of this extra gnawing material also helps to minimize the risk of the birds doing damage to any of the wooden parts used in the construction of the aviary.

All kinds of perches will need to be renewed periodically and the breeder must ensure that they are always firmly fixed. It should be noted that perches for Cockatiels should be considerably greater in diameter than those used for Budgerigars or Canaries.

A wide range of materials can be used to build new aviaries suitable for keeping and breeding Cockatiels; existing buildings of various kinds can also easily be adapted for this purpose. Before starting on an aviary the breeder must consider whether colony or single pair control breeding is to be carried out. It is also advisable to find out from the local government offices if there are any restrictions regarding the erection of a building in the garden.

If the breeder has decided to go in for serious color production then the single pair method must be used to give complete control over each breeding pair. The only way in which the pedigrees of the young can be guaranteed beyond question is by having only one breeding pair to a compartment. Incidentally, it has been found that although Cockatiels are gregarious they will produce a great number of young when the pairs are separate but within sight or hearing range of other pairs. Each flighted or unflighted compartment should not be less than 75 cm (2 ft 6 in) in width so that the birds can fly freely.

An uncontrolled flighted aviary solely for Cockatiels or for a mixed collection of birds need only be of simple design consisting of a sleeping and feeding shelter and an outside wire flight. The sleeping part should be well constructed, free from dampness and drafts. Incidentally, Cockatiels do not require any heat during the winter months. The wire flight itself can be covered with either ordinary wire mesh or the welded wire mesh. When only Cockatiels are to be kept 1·8 cm (¾ in) or 2·5 cm (1 in) mesh will be quite suitable for these larger birds. With a mixed collection 1·3 cm. (½ in) or 1·7 cm (⅝ in) mesh should be used. If heavy gauge wire is used and given a coat of waterproof paint it will have a very long, useful life.

Many breeders have found that if a portion of the top of the wired flight next to the sleeping quarters is covered with clear fiber-glass or plastic sheeting the birds can enjoy the flight during wet and snowy weather. If the upper sides are also covered with clear plastic there is a great advantage during rough weather and the protection will be approved by both adult and young birds.

The floor of the sleeping quarters and the flight should be made as secure as possible against the intrusion of vermin. Close heavy wooden boards, concrete, or precast stone slabs can be used for covering the floor of the sleeping quarters and the wire flight can be grassed over, or covered with fine gravel and sand, or composed of a combination of grass and gravel areas. The inroads of possible vermin can be prevented to a great extent by sinking an "L" shaped strip of small mesh 1·3 cm (½ in) wire netting about 20 cm (8 in) into the ground completely around the entire aviary. This will keep out all rats and the majority of mice except the very small ones which can be exterminated before they have time to grow and breed. Mice in an aviary can disturb nesting birds and foul the seed and water thereby causing a health hazard. The mouse baits obtainable at pet stores are most effective in destroying the odd raiding mouse which may find its way into an aviary.

The perches in the wire flight should be arranged so they look decorative and at the same time give the birds the maximum amount of flying space. Should the flight be grassed then the portion beneath the perches should be cut away and filled with sand or gravel for easy cleaning. Any type of perches can be used in the sleeping quarters, but here again they must be firmly fixed and not placed directly above seed, grit, or water dishes. This precaution applies equally to aviaries, pens, and cages, and it is really a matter of basic common sense. The seed dishes themselves should be good, solid utensils that will stand firmly on a shelf, table, or the floor, and they can be made of pottery, earthenware, glass, or galvanized metal. The bird keeper should place the necessary vessels in the best positions for easy accessibility both for the birds and for the keeper.

Some very useful series of control breeding pens constructed in older buildings such as garden sheds, garages, stables, conservatories, and verandahs have been seen. All that is required in aviary structures such as these is a thorough cleaning, redecorating, and the installation of wire pens. It is usually advisable to have the pens about 2 m (6 ft. 6 in.) high with wire tops to facilitate the catching of the birds. The size and number of pens per structure will be controlled by the breeder's requirements with the width not less than 1 m (3 ft), always bearing in mind that the dangers of limited space which can adversely affect breeding. Perching, seed, water, and grit dishes can be the same as those used in flighted aviaries. Certain buildings are suitable for conversion into flighted aviaries by simply adding a flight on to one side, and with a little thought on the part of the owner these can usually be made most attractive.

Although it may not be the most successful method of

breeding Cockatiels, they do nevertheless reproduce in cages with reasonable freedom. The use of breeding cages will give fanciers who have limited aviary space at their disposal the opportunity of breeding their birds under complete control. The birds should only be housed in such cages for the breeding period and at other times they should have the freedom of pens or flights. If birds are kept in cages all the time they tend to deteriorate in general quality and in breeding potential. Cages for housing a single breeding pair or half a dozen birds for steadying down for exhibition purposes should be approximately 1.3 m (4 ft) in length by .6 m (2 ft) wide and 1 m (3 ft) high.

To make the best use of the internal space in cages the nest boxes should be hung on the side walls of the cages. This will help to make inspection of the nests easy, and during the non-breeding periods the entrance holes through the sides of the cages can be covered with hinged flaps. If bird-room space is very limited the nest boxes can be hung onto the wire fronts, but wherever possible the sides should be used even if it means having one less tier of cages. The perches should be fixed as far apart as convenient to leave sufficient space so that the tails and flights of the birds do not rub against the sides. Nest boxes of the same type can be used for cages, pens, and aviaries.

In recent years the number of Cockatiels kept as single household pets has grown considerably as more and more people discover their charm. They will live quite contentedly in the usual round or square all wire Parrot cages or in wire fronted box cages. A bird desired as a pet should be taken into a household as soon as it can feed on its own, which varies from seven to eight weeks after hatching.

The best time to obtain a bird for training is during the spring and summer months when most suitable young birds are for sale. If it can be arranged, the new bird should be taken home early in the day to give it the maximun amount of time to settle down in its new quarters before nightfall. During the first few hours the bird should be left quietly on its own so that it can explore its new cage and settle in without disturbance. After a few days a bird will usually adjust contentedly and the owner can then start to teach it to talk, first its name and then short uncomplicated sentences. Once a bird is finger tame it can be allowed the freedom of a room and can be taught to perform simple tricks with its toys. As a general rule cock birds are considered the best for training as talking pets but a number of hens will also fulfill this commitment. Cockatiels can be recommended as pets for both adults and young people.

Hang the cuttlefish bone on the side of the cage, within easy reach to your Cockatiel and away from contamination. Photo by N. Richmond.

3.

Feeding

Their simple food requirements are an attractive feature in the keeping and breeding of Cockatiels and one that definitely helps to encourage their culture. Cockatiels thrive and breed well on an easily prepared diet of

Handfeeding enhances the taming process greatly.
Photo by E. Goldfinger.

seeds. The principle seed mixture consists of mixed millets, canary seeds, oats, mixed sunflower seeds, some hemp, and panicum millet. Millet sprays which are ears of the small yellow millet seeds, are greatly enjoyed by both old and young birds at all times of the year. When young birds have just left their nests millet sprays will be found most useful in helping to get them to feed on their own more quickly. Millet sprays can also be helpful when training Cockatiels for exhibition purposes. Some breeders soak millet sprays in cold water for twenty-four hours when using them at breeding times. However, giving birds millet sprays dry avoids any possibility of them going moldy. Whether they are given soaked or dry is a matter for breeders to decide for themselves.

A regular supply of various fresh green foods is most essential for maintaining the stock in a fit, healthy, and vigorous condition throughout the year. Cockatiels will eat and enjoy such green foods as chickweed, seeding grasses, spinach, lettuce, cabbage hearts, brussels sprouts, water cress, shepherd's purse, chicory, and slices of apples and carrots. All green food should be obtained from known clean sources and given fresh daily. Any uneaten food should be removed before it becomes stale or moldy. Cockatiels must always have access to ample supplies of grit, cuttlefish bone, and mineral blocks to maintain themselves in good health and perfect feather. Further mineral elements can be found in crushed dried domestic hens eggshells, river and sea sand, chalk, and old mortar rubble.

Individual breeders have their own ideas as to the best seed mixtures for their birds but they should all contain not less than 40 percent of canary seed. Some 25 percent of mixed sunflower seeds should be added to the canary seed and the remaining 35 percent of the mixture made up of mixed millets, clipped oats, and a small quantity of hemp seed. Hemp, like sunflower seed, contains a high oil content and consequently must be given only in limited quantities which can be increased slightly during the cold winter months.

At breeding times and during the molting periods Cockatiels will benefit considerably from being given soft food. Soft food can take the form of a mixture of equal parts of cod liver oil food (as used for Canaries) and a good insectivorous food. If the birds do not accept the 50:50 ratio the owner can adjust the proportions until the correct balance to their liking is found. Sometimes as a variation wholemeal bread moistened with plain water, boiled milk, honey water, or glucose and water can be offered. Any uneaten soft food should be removed from cages, pens, or aviaries at the end of each day to prevent the possibility of any sour or stale food being

A piece of green food is always welcomed by Cockatiels. For safety, never give your pet any greens picked from the wild. Photo by R. Hansen.

eaten by the birds. Single pet birds will also benefit from being given a little soft food or moistened wholemeal bread periodically, especially during their molting periods.

All Cockatiels like to bathe and facilities should always be provided for them to do so whenever they wish. Large, flat, shallow dishes, preferably of earthenware, should be given for this purpose in addition to their normal drinking vessels.

If it is not possible to have a bathing dish in a pet bird's cage then a fine bird spray will be found a valuable aid and its regular use beneficial to and much appreciated by the bird. However, when a pet bird becomes really tame the bathing problem can easily be overcome by letting the bird bathe in the kitchen sink or in the bathroom. Tame birds have been seen having a fine time under a slow dripping *cold* water tap.

Water for drinking purposes can be given in vessels similar to those used for seed or in clip-on water containers and water fountains. Water fountains are most useful in aviaries and the clip-on containers in pens and cages, and in all cases these should be placed clear of perches and away from the seed and grit dishes.

Mixed grits are best given in flat dishes and should not be mixed with other mineral elements such as old mortar rubble, chalk, or crushed dried domestic hens eggshells. These latter materials should, when given, be in separate dishes. Pieces of both cuttlefish bone and mineral blocks should be firmly fixed so that the birds can gnaw them quite easily.

4.

Breeding

Cockatiels are universally considered to be one of the most free breeding members of the Parrot-like species. Their general breeding management can be on the same lines as prescribed by breeders of Budgerigars.

Compatible individuals are best for breeding.
Aggressive birds can harm each other during courtship.
Photo by W. Wallace.

It is essential that only fully mature birds of the best quality be used for breeding purposes if the strain is to be a viable one. Cockatiels will, if allowed, attempt to breed before they are twelve months old but the use of immature birds is only courting disaster at a later date. The best breeding results are achieved by refraining from using birds in the breeding quarters until they are not less than eighteen to twenty-four months old. Such matured birds can be expected to produce fit, healthy young for four or five seasons.

Birds that are closely related should not be put together for breeding as this inbreeding of stock can lead only to the production of inferior young. In fact, inbreeding should be carried out only by fully experienced breeders who have special knowledge of such matters and have a definite objective in view.

Whenever possible the initial stock of birds should be unrelated and procured from widely separated breeding studs. If these birds are not ringed with either closed or split rings the new owner should do so on receipt of the birds. Both metal and plastic split rings can be obtained at pet shops for this purpose. Should the breeder be a little apprehensive about using closed metal rings which are, of course, a permanent record, then split ones can be used instead. Rings not only serve the purpose of identifying the birds but they also allow the breeder to make and keep positive breeding records. When stock birds are first received their ring number or ring color should be entered in a stud breeding register together with any other particulars. Within a few seasons the owner will have a complete picture of the history of the stock inscribed in the register. This will enable the breeder to mate the stock without any problems caused by close inbreeding or a mistake in any split characters that may be carried by the birds.

Two of these young Cockatiel chicks are Albinos. They completely lack black pigments, but the red cheek patch and yellow color will develop later. Photo by R. Kaehler.

Young Cockatiels can be ringed with closed numbered and year-dated metal rings when they are between six and ten days of age making a permanent positive identification of each bird. The same method of ringing as used for Budgerigars can be employed with Cockatiels. The chick to be ringed is held in the hand with one leg between the thumb and first finger, the three longest toes are brought together and the ring slipped over them along the shank and over the small hind toe. The small toe is then pulled free of the ring with the aid of a sharpened matchstick or similar object. Although the chicks may squeak quite a lot while being ringed it is from the indignity of being handled and not from being hurt. If nests of chicks are to be identified on sight they can be ringed with colored plastic rings at the same time the closed rings are put on. Colored plastic rings are of great value in helping the breeder to pick out special birds in the flights without having to catch and handle them.

The majority of fit, healthy, fully mature Cockatiels are ready to start breeding in the spring about the beginning of March. This is certainly a good time to start as the days are growing longer and warmer, and the supply of various fresh green foods which are very important is becoming far easier to obtain. The methods of breeding practice seem to be divided into two schools of thought; those who like to leave their mated pairs together all the time and the others who split up the pairs at the end of each breeding season. When the pairs are separated the sexes are kept apart in flights until they are required the following breeding season. Here again, this is the same practice followed by most Budgerigar breeders.

When it comes to color breeding the pairs are best split up and the sexes kept strictly apart. This not only al-

A beautiful representative of the Normal Grey or wild-colored Cockatiel. Photo by N. Richmond.

lows the breeder to keep strict control of the birds but also prevents the possibility of unwanted chance cross pairings. In addition, breeders invariably want to make experimental pairings with the available stock and for this reason it is essential that there be no doubt as to the parentage of any birds used.

Before the actual breeding season begins the prospective pairings should be made on paper and then each bird's pedigree checked against the stock register. This will ensure that the breeder makes the right crosses to give the most satisfactory results and that closely related birds are not mated together. With the matching of color breeding pairs it is extremely important that the pedigrees of *all* birds used, whether normals or mutations, are checked annually.

In aviaries, pens, and cages when mated pairs are left together all through the year the nest boxes can be put in position when the breeder feels the birds are fully fit and ready for breeding. When the pairs have been freshly mated it is best to wait some five to seven days before actually giving them their nest boxes. This provides the pairs with plenty of time to get properly acquainted, settle down, mate, and get in the right mood for successful reproduction.

When the matched pairs are fully adult, fit, and ready for breeding it is usual for clutches of eggs to start appearing in the nest boxes fifteen to twenty days after they have been brought together. The number of eggs per clutch can range from three to ten, with the larger clutches being produced mostly by the older mature hens. The eggs are glossy white, oval in shape and vary from 26 to 28 mm by 19 to 21 mm in size. Like Budgerigars, Cockatiels lay their eggs on alternate days which means that there is a difference of a few days between the hatching of the first and last chicks of a nest. The actual length of time is of course governed by whether or not the parents start to sit from the first or subsequent eggs. The incubation period for each egg is twenty-one days. The parent birds take equal care of the broods irrespective of their age and it is extremely rare for the smallest chicks in a nest to come to any harm.

Newly hatched Cockatiel chicks are ugly little things covered with long yellowish silky down. It is not until they start to feather that they really look like birds. Both members of breeding pairs take their turn at incubating the eggs with the cock birds sitting during the day and their partners the night shift. The sexes share equally the duty of feeding their young but cock birds do not seem to feed their mates while the young are in their nests. They appear to think it a waste of time to feed their hens who then have to pass it on to the young when they can feed the chicks just as well direct. When it comes to the breeder inspecting the nest boxes Cockatiels do not mind provided this is not done too frequently. It is very rarely that a pair will desert their eggs or chicks as a protest against the interference with their nests.

There are various types of nest boxes that can be used for Cockatiels, and the favorites with most breeders are the upright and flat types. The approximate dimensions of the upright type are 38 cm (15 in) deep, 25 cm (10 in) wide and long, with a 6 cm (2 in) square or round entrance hole near the top. A good firm perch should be fixed just below the entrance and an inspection door on the top. The dimensions of the flat type are 25 cm (10 in) deep by 25 cm (10 in) wide and 38 cm (15 in) long with the entrance hole and perch at one side and the inspection door on the top. These measurements can of course be varied somewhat if it suits the breeder's particular requirements. It is wise, although not definitely essential, to have loose concave bottoms which should be covered with a good layer of peat, coarse pine sawdust, soft wood shavings or chips, or a mixture of these materials.

Young Cockatiels are fully feathered and ready to leave their nest boxes when they are approximately five weeks old, and because of the difference in their hatching times a number of days pass before the entire brood has flown. The young birds are fed by their parents for a week or ten days after they have left the nest, but they should not be moved from their breeding quarters until the owner is quite certain that they can adequately fend for themselves. Both before and after the chicks have been taken from their parents they must always have access to plenty of the usual seed, millet sprays, grits, and various fresh green foods.

Birds, including Cockatiels, regularly preen their own or each other's feathers. Preening keeps the feathers oiled and in good-looking appearance. Photo by W. Wallace.

5.

Normal Greys

In this and the following Chapters I shall be giving color descriptions of both cocks and hens of some different types. Detailed descriptions of the areas of color enable readers to visualize the birds more clearly when they are

The white-marked wing that is characteristic of a Normal Grey Cockatiel is very evident here. Note the leg band on the bird's foot, too. Photo by N. Richardson.

looking at the color plates and drawings which appear on other pages in this book.

Cock: The general overall color of body consists of various shades of gray with the deepest tones being on the underside of the long pointed tail and with the two center feathers being the palest shade of gray. Front of head, cheeks, and throat are lemon yellow, and the outward curving crest about 2.5 to 3 cm (1 in to 1¼ in) in length is a mixture of yellow and gray. The sides of the crown are white and the large ear patches are red orange. On each wing there is a broad white bar tinted with very pale yellow running from the shoulders across the secondary wing coverts. Eyes are brown. Beaks, feet, and legs are various shades of gray. Overall length including long tail is about 33 cm (13 in).

Hen: General body color is much like the cock with the ear patches not so extensive or as rich in color and the wing bars less pure in color. The white on the crown is absent and the yellow areas are only very faintly tinted and tend to be more grayish in shade. The thighs are barred with pale yellow, and the underside of the tail is striped and dappled with gray and yellow. The overall gray coloring is less pure than on the cock and can have a faint brownish wash. With well matured hens the general color often deepens quite considerably and it becomes more difficult to distinguish them from first year cocks.

Immature Birds: These are paler editions of the hen but they do not get yellow on their facial area until they are about six months old and they do not assume full adult coloring until several months later. Nest feathered Cockatiels are rather difficult to sex. Although those with the brightest colors usually turn out to be cocks this should not be taken as a sure guide to their sex.

The present races of domesticated Cockatiels derived from the wild type birds are invariably more substantially built than the newer mutant colors and consequently are used quite extensively for outcrossing. There are many first class strains of pure normals from which exhibition birds are derived. By carefully selecting the parent birds, the overall substance and general depth of color can be steadily improved. In fact it is the only way in which a strain of any color can be developed and the quality maintained.

Most Cockatiels that are taken into households as pets are of the Normal Grey type although all colors are equal in their potentials as tame and often talking pets.

Except for a chance mutation or mutant colors being carried unbeknown to the breeder pairs of Normal Greys will give only gray colored offspring. Much cross-pairing does take place for the sake of improvement of stock and second and third generation birds are often disposed of as Normals.

Water should always be on hand for Cockatiels. They drink a lot and love bathing. Photo by E. Goldfinger.

6.

Albino Cockatiels

This is a mutation that quickly caught the imagination of many breeders of Parrot-like birds because of its drastic color difference to the Normal Grey. They have

*Above: You can train your pet Cockatiel to perform simple tricks, like pecking or "kissing" you . . . but be careful. Photo by N. Richmond. **Facing page:** Full-length photo of an Albino Cockatiel. Photo by M. Gilroy.*

been incorrectly called Lutinos and sometimes Yellows or Whites by breeders according to the amount of yellow suffusion in their plumage. In actual fact they must be Albinos as Cockatiels are white ground birds like the Blue including Grey series in Budgerigars. However, Normal Grey Cockatiels do show varying amounts of yellow suffusion on their bodies and have red-orange ear patches. When the Albino character is added to their genetical makeup it removes all the dark coloring from their plumage. This character has no effect on yellow and red colors in birds as these are due to entirely different pigments, and it therefore produces White (Albino) birds with different amounts of yellow suffusion and red-orange ear patches. The retention of this yellow pigment did at first cause some breeders to think the birds must be Lutinos or Yellows especially when certain specimens showed an extra amount of suffusion. It may be possible by careful selection of breeding stock that show considerable yellow suffusion to increase further the depth and extent of the yellow areas. Nevertheless, no matter how much the yellow is increased these birds will still remain genetically Albinos.

Cock: The general overall color is pure white in the areas that are gray in the normal form. The front of the head, part of the cheeks and the throat lemon yellow. The crest is a mixture of yellow and white. Ear patches are the normal red-orange shade. The wings have areas of yellow and there is a yellow wash on the tail. Eyes are red. The beak is a yellow horn color. Feet and legs are flesh pink.

Hen: General coloring is much the same as the cock with a yellow wash on the thighs and under the tail.

Immature Birds: These show less yellowing than the adults and are difficult to sex until fully matured. Their

Be sure that your Cockatiel has its wing feathers clipped short before allowing it to leave the cage. New feathers develop after molting, and they should be kept from growing too long. Photo by W. Wallace.

eye color is a brighter and lighter shade of red than that of adults. Even some fully adult Albinos are difficult to sex and this can only be done by carefully watching their behavior towards each other.

The appearance of the Albino mutation added a new interest to the breeding of Cockatiels as the character that causes the color is sex linked in its manner of inheritance. By the use of a sex linked mutation the breeder can control the sex of the colors produced by making certain pairings. This knowledge is most useful when young cock birds are needed for training as tame talking pets.

7.

Pearled Cockatiels

The arrival of the Pearled mutation was rather an unexpected happening as it is a change of feather pattern something like the Opaline in Budgerigars and not a

Above: A fully-tamed Pearled Cockatiel sitting confidently on its keeper's hand. Photo by W. Wallace. **Facing page:** Back view of a Pearled Cockatiel. Photo by W. Wallace.

change of color. This new mutation was called Pearled by the original breeders and it is certainly a most appropriate name for this very attractive variety.

Cock: Colored somewhat like the Normal Grey but with large areas of the wing feathers having two shades of grey coloring making a definite attractive pattern combination. This pattern on the wings is very much like that seen on the Opaline Budgerigars and like them is variable in its markings and the sex-linked nature of its inheritance. The orange-red color of the ear patches and the yellow suffusion on various areas do not seem to be quite so intense as on the Normal Grey. Eyes are clear brown. Beak gray. Feet and legs differing tones of gray sometimes with a pinkish undertone.

Hen: General body color is much like that of the cock with the ear patches not so extensive or as rich and the wing bars are less pure in color. The white on the crown is absent and the yellow areas a little fainter than the cock. The thighs are barred with pale yellow and the underside of the tail is striped and dappled with clear gray and yellow.

Immature birds: These are somewhat paler than the adults with the pattern markings less clear and more variable in their distribution.

8.
Cinnamon Cockatiels

With the domestication of most species of birds there appears sooner or later a Cinnamon form in the yellow ground birds and a Fawn form in the white ground birds. Fawns (Cinnamons) were actually reported to

A Cinnamon Cockatiel. Photo by Brian Seed.

A cage that can be hung provides greater security if you happen to have other pets, like a dog or cat, in your house, too. Photo by W. Wallace.

have been bred a considerable time ago but details and live specimens were not available until recent years. This mutation is known in Europe as Cinnamon and Isabelle but because they are white ground birds they should really be termed "fawn" like the Canaries and Zebra Finches where a white ground is involved. Just when the Fawn mutation first appeared does not seem to have been recorded although examples have turned up in Australia, America, and Europe during the last twenty-five years or so. The actual color of Fawn Cockatiels is more of a gray-brown than the cinnamon-brown shade which is commonly met with in some of the other domesticated birds.

Cock: General overall color of body is various shades of grayish-brown with the deepest tones being on the underside of the long pointed tail and the two central feathers being the palest shade. The front of the head, cheeks and throat are lemon-yellow and the outward curving crest about 2.5 to 3 cm (1 in to 1¼ in) in length is a mixture of yellow and grayish-brown. The sides of the crown are white and the large ear patches are red-orange. On each wing there is a broad white bar tinted with pale yellow running from the shoulders across the secondary wing coverts. Eyes are brown. The beak is a grayish-horn color. Feet and legs are pinkish.

Hen: General body color is much like the cock with the ear patches not so extensive or as rich in color and the wing bars less pure in color. The white on the crown is absent and the yellow areas are only faintly tinted and tend to be more grayish-brown in shade. The thighs are barred with yellow and the underside of the tail is striped and dappled with grayish-brown and yellow. With well matured hens the general color often deepens considerably and it may become difficult to distinguish them from first year cocks.

Immature birds: These are paler editions of the hen but they do not get yellow on their facial area until they are several months old and do not assume full adult coloring until the eighth to tenth month.

9.
Pied Cockatiels

For many years it had been the hope of breeders that they would be able to produce Pied or, as they are sometimes called, Variegated Cockatiels especially as birds were being bred that had extra odd white feathers

*Above: The color pattern of a Pied Cockatiel is rarely bilaterally symmetrical. Photo courtesy of Vogel park Walsrode. **Facing page:** A Pied or Variegated Cockatiel. Photo by N. Richmond.*

in their plumage. However, these mismarked specimens did not produce the desired Pied birds and it was not until a mutation appeared that Pied strains were finally established. The character that gives the broken color appearance is a recessive one and can be carried by other colors, both cocks and hens in "split" form.

Cock: Colored similarly to the Normal Grey with varying sized irregular shaped clear patches of white and yellow tinted white, breaking the dark color. The clear areas vary in size with individual specimens with some birds having quite small patches while others are quite extensively marked although the majority of birds seem to have a 50:50 color arrangement. The beak and eyes are as in Normal Grey but the feet and legs may be grey, flesh pink, or a mixture of both.

Hen: Similar to Normal Grey with the plumage broken by white and yellow tinted white areas similar to the cock.

Immature birds: These are somewhat paler editions of the hens but their lines of demarkation in the broken clear areas are not so clearly defined.

10.
Dilute Cockatiels

Most breeds of domesticated birds sooner or later give a Dilute mutation where the coloring is visible only in varying degrees at less than full strength. For some time

A Silver Cockatiel. Note how distinctly paler in coloration this variety is in comparison to the Normal Grey Cockatiel. Photo courtesy of Vogel park Walsrode.

there had been rumors about Dilute or Silver Cockatiels being bred in Europe. It was said that these birds were recessive in their breeding behavior. It is quite possible for a Dilute form to be either a dominant or a recessive breeding type. The birds seen were certainly a paler and brighter shade than the Normal Greys and the color could well be called silver. It is possible that these birds may have been developed by selective pairings of pale Normal Greys over a period of time. Even if they should turn out to be a man made type it would certainly show what can be done in the breeding aviaries with care and perseverance. When sufficient stock becomes available undoubtedly breeding experiments will be carried out and the question of their status answered.

Cock: The general overall color of the body is various shades of bright silvery-gray with the deepest tones being on the underside of the long pointed tail and with the two central feathers being the palest. The front of the head, cheeks and throat are lemon-yellow and the crest is a mixture of yellow and silvery-gray. The sides of the crown are white and the large ear patches red-orange. On each wing there is a broad white bar tinted with pale yellow running from the shoulders across the secondary wing coverts. Eyes are reddish-brown; the beak grayish; feet and legs are pinkish.

Hen: General body color is much like the cock with the ear patches not so extensive or as rich in color and the wing bars less pure in color. The white on the crown is absent and the yellow areas are only faintly tinted and tend to be more silvery-gray in shade. The thighs are barred with yellow and the underside of the tail is striped and dappled with silver-gray and yellow.

Immature birds: These are paler editions of the hen.

11.

Other Color Varieties

When a species has several color mutations it is always possible through a series of matings to produce birds that show the characters of two or more mutations in one bird and Cockatiels are no exception to this rule.

A Pied Cockatiel that is predominantly white and yellow. Variegation is limited to a small area of the wings. Photo courtesy of Vogel park Walsrode.

Some Cockatiel owners recommend the use of vitamin supplements to provide their birds the best nutrition possible. Photo by W. Wallace.

The one existing mutation which does not visually combine with others is the Albino and this is because of its overall loss of dark coloring. The Pied can be bred in Fawn (Cinnamon), Pearled and Dilute forms and it is possible to have Pied Fawn (Cinnamon) Pearled, Pied Fawn (Cinnamon) Dilute and Pied Pearled Dilute. The Pearled can be had in Pearled Fawn (Cinnamon), Pearled Dilute and Pearled Fawn (Cinnamon) Dilute.

The Dilute (Silver) character can also be used to create further attractively colored varieties such as Dilute (Silver) Pearled, Dilute (Fawn), Dilute (Silver) Pied, Dilute (Silver) Pearled Fawn, Dilute (Silver) Pied Fawn, Dilute (Silver) Pied Pearled, and Dilute (Silver) Pied Pearled Fawn. By including the Dilute (Silver) character in composite forms the resulting birds have softer shades of color throughout making them distinct from the ordinary gray shade. When the Fawn (Cinnamon) character is included then birds of a somewhat paler and altered color tone are produced. Because of the basic color of Cockatiels the present mutant colors will be a little paler than the Normal but nevertheless clearly discernible. From this it will be seen that since the number of mutations has increased there can be a very considerable number of different colors and combinations of the Cockatiel. It should be noted that many of the composite forms mentioned in this chapter have yet to be produced by the enterprising breeder. With further possible mutations coming along color breeding in Cockatiels will be a most exciting part of bird breeding.

Your pet Cockatiel will certainly be entertained by a small mirror and a bell. Photo by V. Serbin.

12.
The Pet Cockatiel

As each year passes, the number of Cockatiels kept purely as house pets increases steadily. People are finding out that Cockatiels are very easy birds to finger tame, and of course their cost is very reasonable when

Above: Like most parrots, a Cockatiel is very efficient in opening hard seeds. Photo by N. Richmond. ***Facing page:*** A cage of different varieties of Cockatiels and two other birds. Photo by N. Richmond.

compared with many other members of the Parrot family. They are certainly attractive to look at and although not very prolific talkers they will learn to repeat a number of words and short sentences.

For training as a tame talking pet it is preferable that a young, fit, healthy cock bird be selected and taken away from the care of its parents as soon as it is seen to be feeding *entirely on its own*. Young hens can also be trained and many will make tame affectionate pets and learn to talk, but young cock birds are less temperamental and learn to talk with greater ease. A prospective pet Cockatiel owner may have to rely on the knowledge of the breeder or pet shop when it comes to sexing a bird.

Your Cockatiel will certainly enjoy picking individual millet seeds from a spray. Millet is also commonly available in loose form. Photo by W. Wallace.

A Normal Grey Cockatiel being coaxed to move from a wood perch to the trainer's forefinger. Photo by N. Richardson.

Before a bird is obtained, a cage which is to be its home for many years should be purchased. A cage can be a box type one of a size to fit in with the furnishing of a room or a more conventional round or square metal wire Parrot-type cage. Ample food, water, and grit vessels must be positioned in the cage together with a piece of cuttlefish bone and a mineral nibble. The cage floor should be covered with bird sand or very fine gravel and cleaned regularly.

It is best to get the new bird early in the day so he has plenty of time to settle down into his new home well before roosting time. If a bird is to be kept in a livingroom that is much used by the family it is advisable to have a fabric covering over part of the cage so the bird is not worried by the movements around. A bird should be allowed at least eight to twelve days to get fully accustomed to his new surroundings before any serious training is started. Any sudden movements or loud noises near the cage must be avoided, and when giving fresh seed and water the bird should be quietly spoken to in a clear even voice. It is most satisfactory for one person in a household to undertake the training in the first instance to help to prevent the bird from being confused by different voice tones.

When the owner feels that a bird has become thoroughly accustomed to its new home, the cage door can be opened and a piece of millet spray or green food offered. While this is being done the tidbit should be slowly pushed towards the bird, holding it steady when he starts to nibble the food. In most cases it is not long before he is eating out of the owner's fingers without any sign of nervousness. The next move is to gradually ease a finger beneath the bird's feet so that he can sit on the finger while nibbling the food from the other hand.

As soon as he is sitting fearlessly he can be slowly pulled towards the open door and out into the room and then back again into the cage. Once the bird has reached such a stage of tameness he will usually let his owner gently stroke his chest and tickle the back of his head.

In due course the cage door can be left open for short periods to allow the bird to fly around the room and get some beneficial exercise. When the bird is at liberty it is essential that all doors and windows are firmly closed and any solid fuel, gas, or electric fires covered. Cut flowers and potted plants of all kinds should be removed from the room while the bird is loose as many green plants attract a bird and if eaten have a bad effect on the bird's digestion.

A pet Cockatiel is very easy to feed with a mixture of sunflower seed, Canary seed, mixed millets, and a few clipped oats. The breeder or pet shop keeper will, if asked, tell the new owner the type of seed mixture the bird has been eating and this is the one that should be used. Cockatiels as a species are extremely fond of various fresh green foods and a list of these will be found elsewhere in this book. Whenever possible a small quantity of green food should be given daily.